Spells *for* Surviving a Haunted Childhood

(PART ONE)

SPELLS FOR SURVIVING A HAUNTED CHILDHOOD
(PART ONE, TWO & THREE)
© 2025 by Haunted Light Productions

ISBN: [979-8-9995861-0-0]

First Edition: 2025

Printed in the United States of America

–My Whole, Haunted Heart–

To my husband-
   Your love has always been the light I didn't know I needed. Thank you for holding space for all my ghosts and being my calm through every storm.

To my children-
   You are the reason I still believe in magic. May you always know your worth and never shrink for anyone. My love for each of you runs deeper than any ocean and reaches farther than any star.

To my friends-
   For those who stayed when things got heavy - you helped me carry what I thought would crush me. I'll never forget your kindness.

And to my therapist-
   Thank you for helping me untangle the darkness, name the wounds, and write new spells for the parts I once tried to hide.

This book is a crucial part of my healing.
   - May it help someone else begin their journey.

Protect Your Mindscape

This is not a fairytale. It's a Grimoire - stitched together from the quiet, aching spells of a childhood that was far from gentle.

Inside, you'll find stories shaped by emotional wounds, generational curses, family heartbreak, abandonment, and moments of harm that should never touch a child. Some chapters speak softly - but honestly - about experiences of trauma, including those that are hard to name, and harder to carry.

It contains first person accounts of childhood trauma, including but not limited to *neglect, abuse (emotional, physical, and sexual), death, abandonment, addiction, and mental illness.* The truths within may be difficult to read - I assure you, they were even harder to live.

Please go gently. If any of these stories echo your own pain, may they also help guide you toward healing. May these meditation style spells bring you comfort and connection. Use this book to reflect on your past and help connect the dots. Cast your own magical healing spells.

If something feels too heavy, it's okay to step away. Breathe. Come back when you're ready - if you're ready.

You are not alone here. You are not broken. I hope, in these pages, you find more than pain. *I hope you find your light, too.*

I believe in you.

With all my love and magic,
—BARB

The Spell That Starts Them All

Remember, this is *not* a happy fairytale. Truth is there's barely any happiness between these covers.

There are no talking animals to guide you home, no fairy godmothers waiting in the wings. No glass slippers - just shattered things you learn to walk on barefoot and how to disappear into the shadows.

This 'Grimoire' is a book of healing spells woven from old scars. A collection of awful, scary, evil truths the world tried to make me swallow. This book does not flinch. It does not turn away. It is a tale drenched in awful truth, but woven by beautiful magic.

Inside these pages are haunted houses with too many doors, smiles worn like masks, and silence so loud it echoes - decades later.

But this is also a story of perseverance. Of finding small lights in impossible places. Of learning to name the pain, and then cast it into something survivable. Something *sacred*.

Hopefully, you've never known the depths of the pain I've endured. But if any of these stories feel familiar - if they whisper to your forgotten corners of your mind - then I hope the spells tucked between them help you find your way back to yourself.

Piece by piece. Word by word. Heart first, always.

So take a deep breath.
Hold these pages gently.
And let's uncover some magic together, *but only if you believe*.

Let's begin where all the best spells do - with a recalling of old memories.

Spell for Remembering What Was Buried

(For the memories that sank beneath silence)

Ingredients:
One quiet hour
A photograph (or the absence of one)
Dirt from someplace you once called home
A single white candle in your mind
Your voice

Directions:

1. Whisper these words:

> *"What was hidden, what was hushed,*
> *In dust, in silence, in the rush-*
> *I call it now, I call it near,*
> *Without the shame, without the fear."*

2. Speak aloud the first memory that returns to you. Any piece. A scent. A shape. A child's name.

3. Let the candle inside your soul burn until it flickers.

4. When you are ready, say:

> *"What was buried is not gone.*
> *It lives here now, and I live on."*

5. Write down your journey. Express your feelings. Be honest.

Note:

The remembering may arrive slowly. It might speak in dreams. It may ache. That is okay. Keep the dirt. Keep writing. Keep going.

Spells for Surviving a Haunted Childhood
(Part One)

CHAPTER
One

The Blizzard That Swallowed Me Whole

They say the storm came without warning.

But I remember the wind whispering secrets days before it ever howled. Maybe I should've listened harder.

I was three years old - small enough to still believe in fairytales, but old enough to know that sometimes the world can break itself without asking permission.

It happened in the winter of 1993, during the great blizzard that rocked half the nation. But to me, it wasn't just weather. It was a creature - a living thing made of ice and hunger, howling down from the mountains like it had an appetite for little girls who wandered too far.

And it found me.

I stepped outside when no one was watching. Maybe I wanted to taste the air, see if the snowflakes would catch on my tongue. Or perhaps I thought the snow could carry me somewhere quieter than the house behind me - where everyone yelled like it was the only language we knew.

The snow fell fast, so thick the world disappeared.

Somewhere in the swirl, my red mitten - my favorite - slipped from my hand. I reached out for it, but the wind screamed like a thousand voices, carrying it farther, and farther until it vanished in the white blur. It was the first thing I lost, but certainly not the last.

I took a few steps forward, calling out for the mitten like it might come back if I asked nicely. But my voice disappeared into the blizzard. The snow swallowed every sound. My feet sank with each step, the cold biting through the thin soles of my shoes, not fit for winter. I turned to look back at the house.

Panic bloomed in my chest. The quiet kind, tight and fast, like a bird flapping its wings behind my ribs. I couldn't see anything. Not the porch. Not the crooked light that buzzed and flickered above the front steps. Just white. I opened my mouth to yell for someone - *anyone* - but the wind stole the words before they left my lips.

My breath came faster. My legs trembled. The snow was up to my chest now, and it felt like the earth itself wanted to pull me under.

Then something changed.

The wind, so violent just a moment ago, softened. It didn't stop - it *shifted*. It began to swirl around me, gentle now, coaxing rather than cruel. I blinked through frozen lashes and watched as the snowflakes started to *dance* around me.

The panic loosened its grip. My breath slowed. I stood still, one less mitten and shivering, but... unafraid nonetheless. The storm didn't feel like a threat anymore. It felt like a curtain - like something sacred was hiding just behind it, waiting for me to be still enough to notice.

I reached out my hand again - not to try to catch the mitten this time, but to touch the wind itself.

And it touched me back.

At first, I wasn't scared. I just listened. The snow didn't fall - it spoke. It moved around me in slow, deliberate spirals, and I could feel something ancient and watching.

A chill brushed my neck, like breath from a mouth I couldn't see. It knew me. I didn't know how I knew that. I just did.

The chill knew my name.

I could hear it loud and clear. Echoing in my heart, calling out to me. Then, from the tree line, a shape appeared out of thin air.

It was just a shimmer at first - and then, a figure. Tall, wrapped in something heavy that billowed like smoke. I could only see what appeared to be a large, dark cloud that stood out from the whiteout conditions. And it walked without footprints. It moved without sound.

But it was watching me.

Before I could try to move towards it to investigate further, a new sound cut through the storm - the sharp crunch of boots behind me. My uncle. I didn't even hear him coming. His arms wrapped around me suddenly, scooping me up from the snow like I was weightless. His chest was warm and fast-beating, his breath visible in panicked clouds.

"You scared us, little girl," he said, his voice rough in the cold. "Don't ever walk off in the snow like that again."

He turned toward the house and started carrying me back through the storm.

And that's when it happened.

I looked back over his shoulder - and I swear I saw something unexplainable disappear into thin air just beyond the trees.

I never told anyone. Because how do you explain that the storm wasn't the scariest part? It was being seen, truly seen, by something that shouldn't exist.

I didn't know what I saw, but it *saw* me.

Papaw stood in the doorway, his outline golden in the porch light. His arms were open, and his voice was calling me home. The storm raged, but in that moment, Papaw was bigger than the mountain, bigger than the fear. He wrapped me in a blanket and whispered something soft - a promise, maybe - that the cold wouldn't have me.

But I knew the truth.

The cold had seen me. And it had marked me. Not just the chill in the air, but the colder thing behind the trees.

The Chill That Knew My Name.

Spell for Braving the Cold

Ingredients:

One red mitten (even if lost)
Three deep breaths of winter air
A golden thread - for warmth
The memory of a safe voice calling your name

Directions:

1. Close your eyes and breathe deep. Imagine the wind rushing in your ears.

2. Remember the feeling of being small, but not alone.

3. Say this:

> "I remember the snow and the silence,
> and how it tried to take me.
> But I was not swallowed.
> I was seen. I was found.
> I carry warmth in my bones,
> passed down from hands that held me.
> The cold does not get to have me.
> I belong to the light."

Repeat until the snow stops falling inside your heart.

CHAPTER
Two

The House With Too Many Eyes

Some houses don't blink. They stare.

The family compound was stitched together like a crooked quilt - four houses scattered across the hills, all linked by blood and buried grudges.

The house I stayed in most was the one that stared the hardest - Nanny and Papaw's house. Its windows always seemed to be watching, even when the curtains were drawn.

It smelled like mothballs, Aqua Net hairspray, and old rage - the kind of anger that got passed down like antique furniture. The air was heavy, too heavy for a four-year-old's chest. I remember thinking the ceilings were low, not because of the architecture, but because the house was pressing in. Like it was trying to shrink me down to nothing.

And then there were the dolls.

Nanny kept them in a cabinet in the living room, each behind a glass door that clicked shut like a tiny coffin lid. Rows of porcelain girls with ringlet curls, wide smiles, and lace dresses.

Their painted eyes followed you when you moved. Some of them had teeth. I used to wonder if they whispered to each other when the room was dark - little secrets passed mouth to mouth, made of enamel and dust.

I always received a doll for Christmas, specifically from Nanny, even though they always creeped me out. But as quickly as it was unwrapped, it was taken back and locked tight in her hutch with a key.

Nanny said they were valuable. "Don't touch," she snapped the first time she caught me looking. "Those are worth more than you are."

I hadn't even put a finger on the glass.

That day, she snapped at me in front of Papaw - the kind of venom you only spit when you forget a child still has ears. And a heart.

"She needs to go on home," she hissed, not knowing or not caring that I was listening just around the corner. "Like a bruise that never heals. Always crying. Always whining about something. I didn't take her to raise."

Papaw had hushed her. Not with words, but with that deep, gravelly breath he took when he was angry.

It was the only time he seemed bigger than the house. He told Nanny I was to stay at their house tonight, my mom and dad were fighting again, and he didn't want me in the middle of it. Nanny sighed in anguish and frustration.

That night, Papaw tucked me in with a kiss goodnight while Nanny silently disproved from the hallway. I usually slept on the couch at their house so I could watch TV, but tonight it was broken from the fight last week. Nanny threw a shoe and busted the screen.

As I laid in the eerie darkness of their home that night, the sound of Nanny's voice ran in my ears. Am I a bother? Do I cry too much? The air turned colder than it had any right to be. I was covered in blankets, but still shivering through chattering teeth. I somehow fell asleep despite this sudden shiver.

I woke to the sound of the floorboards creaking - not like someone was walking, but like the house itself was settling into a new shape. The air felt strange. Thicker. Wet with silence. Something in the room had changed. I could feel it, like the way animals feel storms before they hit.

And there, on the lip of the hutch that had been empty just yesterday, sat a porcelain doll I'd never seen before. She wasn't locked inside like the others. She was free.

She wasn't one of Nanny's.

She didn't belong.

Tall. Pale. Dressed in a midnight blue gown with tiny black buttons down the front. Her eyes were glass - not painted - and they watched me like she knew things I hadn't learned yet.

Her lips were the color of dried blood, and a fine crack split her porcelain cheek like a secret trying to escape. Suddenly, her left eye dislodged and rolled onto the floor. The sound echoed through the room, spiking my heart rate and a trembling in my hands.

I didn't move.

I didn't dare.

Because I knew - the way you just know things in your bones - that it hadn't been placed there.

It had appeared.

And something else was in the room. Not just this ghostly doll that appeared like the wind.

In the farthest shadow, near the hall closet door, the air bent. Like heat waves rising off asphalt, but cold. A shape that shimmered without light. Feminine, long-limbed, and impossible to hold in place with your eyes.

The Chill That Knows My Name.

It didn't speak. But I felt it thinking. Watching. I knew this was the mysterious figure in the snow. I could hear the doll's porcelain limbs creaking faintly as if flexing for the first time in years. And then, *it was gone.*

The dark figure melted into the wall. The doll stood still as stone. But I couldn't sleep. I pulled the covers over my head, whispering made-up spells to keep my breath warm.

The next morning, Papaw made scrambled eggs. The house pretended nothing had happened. But when I passed the hutch, the doll was there - her eye was still missing. It wasn't a dream after all.

Nanny's voice sliced through the room.

"What did you do?"

"I didn't - I didn't touch her," I whispered.

"You're a liar, just like your mother."

Her words landed like hailstones. I could feel my face burn. She scooped up the doll like it was holy and turned her back to me.

That night, I heard her telling Papaw she was putting the "thing in the attic."

But the missing eye? It was gone. Not in the trash. Not on the floor. Not under the couch. Not tucked into the folds of the doll's dress. Just... *vanished.*

I didn't realize it then - how pieces of my life were starting to go missing. I just remember feeling like something had changed. Like the doll wasn't finished with me.

Like her missing feature had opened something else - not just in porcelain, but in the world.

Spell for When the Gaze Feels Too Heavy

Ingredients:

One blanket pulled tightly over your head
Three soft breaths to calm a racing heart
The sound of your own name, spoken kindly
A memory of someone who saw you without scorn

Directions:

1. Close your eyes and make your body small - not in fear, but in protection.

2. Picture a mirror that only shows the good parts.

3. Whisper:

> "I am not a thing to be stared at.
> I am not a doll or a burden or a mistake.
> I am a child of light,
> even in rooms full of shadow.
> You may watch me, but you will not break me."

Repeat until the air feels safe again.

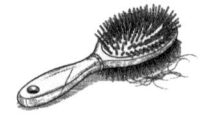

CHAPTER
Three

Inherited Silence

Some women are taught to disappear while they're still standing in the room.

I didn't know that then. I only knew my mother was different when Nanny was around. Stiff. Smaller. Like a shadow of herself, just waiting to be scolded.

Our house sat just down the grassy path from Nanny and Papaw's place. Close enough to hear a screen door slam. Close enough to be called when someone needed something - or someone to blame.

I stayed at my grandparents' house a lot when I was little, especially when things at home got loud. But the air inside always felt... off. A stillness that clung to my skin, even after I left.

Nanny ruled her house with a quiet cruelty. She didn't yell much - she didn't have to. Her words could draw blood just fine without volume.

She was the kind of woman who cut you with an insult, then acted like it was your fault for bleeding.

My mother shrank under her like a shadow pinned to the floor. When Nanny wasn't home, my mother tried. She wasn't perfect - not even close - but there were moments when I could almost believe she was the mom I needed her to be.

She played Barbies with me sometimes, even if she drifted outside halfway through, lighting a smoke out on the porch and staring into the trees.

Her hugs always felt suffocating, like she was squeezing what liveliness she needed *out* of me, not filling me up with the love I desperately craved and deserved.

She took me to a few of my softball practices, hollering my name from the bleachers too loud, too proud - like she was trying to prove something.

Sometimes, she brushed my hair and told me I was beautiful. And most mornings, I woke up and realized she'd forgotten to say goodnight again.

But even those half-bright moments vanished when Nanny entered the room. It was like watching someone perform some twisted version of love until the director walks in and yells, 'cut!'.

Mom would tense, shoulders tight, mouth shut, already bracing for the next blow - even if it came dressed as a sigh.

And I'd sit on the floor with a half-dressed Barbie in my lap, wondering where my mother had gone - and why I suddenly felt like I was alone again.

One night, the tension cracked wide open like an egg against a ceramic bowl.

I was sitting at the kitchen table with a crayon in my hand when it happened - something quiet between them turned mean in an instant.

I don't remember the exact words, but I remember the way they landed. Nanny's voice clashed like ice breaking across the table.

"You've always been so weak," she spat. "Too soft for this world. And now you're raising her to be the same. All she does is cry. She's a waste of space - like mother, like daughter."

It took me a second to realize that *she* was *me*. Wait, *I'm* a waste of space?

Papaw stepped in. His voice rumbled low, but final.

"That's enough," he said, without raising it. "Let the girl be."

Nanny didn't argue. She just turned away, muttering under her breath like she was casting a spell made of disappointment.

That night at home in my bed, I couldn't sleep.

The air in my room held me like a secret. Too heavy for a five-year-old to carry. And that's when I felt it - again.

That presence in the corner. The one I'd known before, even if I didn't have a name for it. A hush colder than the room, like something ancient, had taken interest in me.

The Chill That Knows My Name. Back again.

No fear. Just recognition.

Like it had been watching the whole time, waiting for this

moment to mark me as its own.

Some inherit houses. Some inherit money.

Some of us inherit silence - wrapped in shame, passed down like fine china.

Too precious to break. Too dangerous to use.

And some silences don't stay quiet.

They growl through clenched teeth.

Spell for What You Can't Say Out Loud

Ingredients:

One Barbie, half-dressed
One hairbrush used on half-brushed hair
A silence you mistook for safety
A voice swallowed in your own throat

Directions:

1. Sit quietly and hold what remains.

2. Picture the way her voice used to sound.

3. Say this:

> "I see the effort between the silences.
> I remember when it almost felt like enough.
> Even broken love has a shape - and I can carry
> its outline without letting it shape me.
> I do not disappear. I become."

Repeat until your own voice comes back.

CHAPTER
Four

Keeper of the Light

Before I knew what magic was, I knew what safety felt like. It had the shape of a man with calloused hands and a voice like rain on a tin roof at dawn.

Papaw - Strong. Stable. Secure.

Where Nanny's words sliced, his stitched. Where her presence made the air tighten, his made it expand. I think maybe every storm needs a lighthouse - and he was mine.

He had once worked deep in the coal mines, swallowed by the dark for hours at a time. Maybe that's why he knew how to carry light - because he'd spent so many years making sure he could find his way out of the dark.

When I was small, he retired early - not for rest, but for me. He traded the grind of underground work for something softer but just as vital - watching over me. My valiant protector. While Mom and Dad worked, I spent my days with Papaw.

We were an unlikely pair - one small girl and one quiet mountain man - but we fit. Some souls just do.

Our days had a rhythm, simple and perfect.

We watched old crime shows in the living room, sprawled across hand-me-down couches with faded upholstery.

When the theme songs came on, we'd dance in the kitchen, a silly shoulder bop that made me giggle until I couldn't breathe.

He'd hum along while I twirled like a top, and somehow his steady presence kept the whole world from spinning out of control.

He front porch sat like it was a sacred ritual. He'd rock slowly in his chair, white undershirt catching the golden light of late afternoons, BB gun resting across his lap. Sometimes he'd shoot at bumblebees just to show me he still could - not to kill, just to impress.

Summer had a sound with him - creaking wood, a chorus of cicadas, and the slow exhale of a man who knew exactly where he belonged.

He wore the same thing almost every day - a white shirt and black bottoms. Shorts in the summer. Pants in the winter. Not out of laziness - out of loyalty. To his own rhythm. In his own way.

His consistency was a kind of magic I didn't yet have a name for.

While everything else in my world shifted - moods, houses, the sharp angles of Nanny's affection - Papaw stayed. He stayed in his chair. In his routines. In my heart.

He collected model trains with a devotion that bordered on religious. I never understood the obsession when I was little - all those tiny tracks and wheels. But now I think maybe he loved the order of it. The way the trains always knew where they were going.

The way they came back around, every time.

Spell for Illuminating the Shadows

Ingredients:

The creak of a porch rocking chair
The echo of a theme song in the kitchen
The hum of summer cicadas
A man who always showed up

Directions:

1. Sit in a patch of sunlight, even if it's small.

2. Close your eyes and breathe in the memory of someone who made you feel safe.

3. Say this:

> "I remember the light in the dark.
> I remember hands that steadied
> without squeezing.
> I carry safety in my cells now,
> passed down through steadiness.
> The storm may return -
> but I will always find my way home."

Repeat when the world feels too loud to stay in your body.

CHAPTER
Five

Hello, Darkness

It started with Papaw getting tired.

Not the kind of tired that came after mowing the grass or swatting at bees on the porch. Not the kind of tired that made him sigh and sit down slowly. This was a different kind of tired. Quiet and heavy. The kind that stuck to him like it didn't want to let go.

At first, people said he had a bug. Then they said it was something in his blood. Words like "treatment" and "weak" started showing up in whispers. And one day, he stopped coming out on the porch altogether.

His room became something sacred and strange. I wasn't allowed to run barefoot inside anymore. There were machines now. Humming and ticking and beeping. Tubes and things that didn't belong in a house like theirs. I remember peeking through the crack in the door, holding my breath, watching him sleep. He looked like a version of Papaw that had been left out in the rain.

Mom would tell me, "He's just resting. He needs all his strength."

28

But Papaw *was* strength. And watching it leak out of him made the whole house feel wrong.

He called for me once, soft and hoarse. I heard my name come out of his mouth like it cost him something. But I couldn't move. My feet stayed glued to the mauve carpet. I was afraid that if I went in, I wouldn't come out the same.

I whispered, "I love you," and ran.

The next day, they pulled me from class. I was sitting in a plastic chair, talking about the latest, sliced rainbow bread with a classmate. The intercom crackled, and the secretary's voice asked me to come to the front office.

I knew before I got there. The hallway felt too long. Too quiet.

Mom stood in the office, her face pale, makeup streaked. Her eyes didn't meet mine quite right.

"Baby," she said, crouching down. "He's gone."

My stomach dropped. Not like falling. Like vanishing. Like part of me just turned to air. It was a long walk to the truck and an even longer drive home.

—

The funeral was too bright. That strange kind of light that makes everything look smaller.

The pews were full of faces I didn't know. The flowers made me dizzy. I hated my tights. I'll never forget the smell.

My papaw's sweet face, longing for him to wake from this

nightmare. It wasn't fair. This whole funeral was just teasing me. Everyone proclaimed he had passed away, but here he was, right in front of me. Just. Wake. Up.

I sat in my father's lap, stiff in his suit. His warmth was the only thing I recognized at that moment. He held me close, almost as if he was saying, 'Just stay with me, you'll be okay'.

I closed my eyes. And when I opened them, the air suddenly shifted. The room was darker. Everything felt heavy. Then I realized I wasn't sitting on my father's lap anymore.

The cold had come. But not like before.

This time it didn't crawl. It didn't bite. It wasn't menacing or hiding.

This time it held me.

Wrapped around me like a shawl. A hush. A darkness that knew my name and didn't demand anything from me.

Hello darkness, my old friend...

I didn't know I was humming until my mother nudged my back with her elbow. I stopped. The moment broke. The dark pulled away, waiting, just beyond the edge of the stained glass.

It watched. It remembered. It waited.

Papaw was gone. And the warmth of our family went with him.

The porch went quiet.

The bumblebees flew without fear.

Nanny went sharper. Louder. Harder.

But that would come later.

For now, I sat in the cold, knowing something had changed inside me, allowing my darkness to watch from a close distance.

A seed had been planted. And it didn't bloom in the sunlight.

Spell for When the Light
Leaves the Room Too Soon

Ingredients:

A candle burnt out with much more life to give
One folded blanket, heavy with memory
The final word you never got to say
A sliver of childhood, quietly cracked

Directions:

1. Sit in the quietest part of your home.

2. Wrap the blanket around your shoulders - even if it no longer holds warmth

3. Hold the unlit candle in your hands.

4. Whisper the name of the one you lost, three times.

5. Let the silence answer.

> "I carry you in the hush between heartbeats.
> I name the absence
> so it doesn't swallow me whole.
> I let the darkness sit beside me -
> but I do not hand it the reins."

Repeat whenever the darkness becomes blinding.

CHAPTER
Six

The Doll That Didn't Belong

Papaw had been gone a few weeks when the house started feeling colder, not just in temperature, but in the way shadows stretched longer, how footsteps echoed sharper. His chair on the porch stayed empty, rocking gently in the breeze like it missed the weight it once held.

Mom stopped talking. Nanny got louder.

She cooked more often, but not out of love. It was a performance. Every stir of the spoon had a bite to it. She snapped at Mom for blinking wrong, for not being fast enough, for breathing too loudly. And Mom just took it. She would fold into herself like laundry being pressed with a hot iron.

One afternoon, I wandered into Papaw's old room while no one was watching. It still smelled like him - peppermint, pipe smoke, and a hint of sawdust. I climbed onto the bed and buried my face in his pillow, trying to find the shape of him in the cotton.

That's when I saw it.

Tucked behind a cracked shoebox, under a faded flannel shirt, was something strange, a glimmer that caught my attention. It was a glass eye. A familiar one. But where have I seen this before?

Wait a minute! This was the eye from the doll that appeared out of thin air. But how?

I pocketed it, curious more than anything, and jetted to the basement to hide it from sight. Nanny hated the basement. I placed it in a tissue, folded it just right, and hid it from the world.

Later that week, the doll reappeared. I couldn't tell you when, but it wasn't there one day, and suddenly it was.

It came without warning in Nanny's hutch. Delicate. Unsmiling. Dressed in a stiff lace dress, pale and perfect. But I knew every doll in that case by heart - and this *DEFINITELY* wasn't hers.

I stared at it, my heart beating strangely. She was tucked so tightly behind the rows of other figures, like she didn't belong, but not in an obvious way. Almost invisible. But I knew. I had seen this broken doll before. That night. But it was not *inside* the hutch.

Then I realized. The eye. Yes! It *had* to mean something!

I ran to where I'd hidden it, maybe fixing it would connect me to him, somehow, some way. Stranger things had happened.

I ran downstairs - I searched in the back of a forgotten drawer - but it was gone. It wasn't unusual for my keepsakes to be moved or taken while here. I learned not to question it. There was no 'mine' at Nanny's house.

She cornered me that evening, "You broke it, I just know

it," she hissed. "Don't you lie to me, little girl."

I shook my head, eyes wide. "I didn't-"

"You always were a sneaky thing. Just like your mother. I found the eye you hid. I know you broke it. The whole thing's garbage now."

I opened my mouth to defend her. Or maybe to defend myself. But no words came.

Nanny opened the hutch and grabbed the doll by the neck. She stormed off, slamming the doll into the trash can just before she exited the room.

That night, I sat on my bed, fists clenched around nothing. The missing eye was gone. She must have found it and blamed me for hiding it. But I *knew* it had meant something. That it was more than coincidence.

Only now I'd never know why.

Spell for When You Aren't Believed

Ingredients:

One missing piece
A truth no one heard
A closed door
An empty folded tissue (tear soaked is fine)

Directions:

1. Hold the truth in your palm like a stone.

2. Whisper it into the dark three times.

3. Breathe in silence. Breathe out shame.

> "I know what I saw. I know what I held.
> Even if no one else believes me - I do.
> I know the truth."

Repeat until your voice returns.

CHAPTER
Seven

Runaway Train

After Papaw died, it was like Nanny wanted to erase him.

Gone were the model trains that lined the walls of their bedroom. Gone were his BB guns and his fishing pole propped behind the shed. One day they were there, and the next, the shelves were bare. The porch felt hollow without its usual creak under his weight.

She said it was too painful to see his things lying around, but the speed with which she discarded them made the rest of us feel like grief had turned her hands into garbage disposals.

She donated boxes to the church without telling anyone. Hauled bags to the dump in the back of her old Buick. Claimed she was "cleaning up," but it felt more like she was cutting him out of the house like rot.

The rest of the family all assumed we'd each be given something. A flannel shirt. A favorite model train. Even just one of the pocketknives he used to carry, worn smooth from years in his palm. But no one received a single thing.

"Nobody wants his old junk, it's garbage," she snapped when my uncle asked about Papaw's train sets. Her eyes were sharper than ever. Her voice was mean in new ways. Grief had hardened her, made her brittle and cold, like frost that doesn't melt.

Mom cried on the walk home one evening. Not loud sobs - just quiet, leaky tears that slid down her cheeks as she stared towards the road. She had hoped for something, too. Anything.

"He promised me that watch when I was little," she whispered. "He said it would be mine one day."

But the watch was gone. Everything was.

I wandered the house when Nanny wasn't paying attention, searching the corners, hoping maybe something had been missed. A button. A tool. A leftover smell.

All I found was dust.

She was different after he passed. Meaner. She snapped at everyone, especially Mom. Her words got heavier, too, like they were dipped in lead. There was no more patience, no more pretending.

One night, I heard them yelling in the kitchen. Which was rare. My mom *never* yelled back.

"You don't know what real loss is," Nanny hissed.

"How could you say that? He was my dad!" my mother shouted back.

Nanny slammed a cupboard. "And my husband. Mine. You don't get to tell me how to grieve."

I stood in the hallway, holding my breath. It was the first time I realized losing someone could mean you lose more than one person.

The house never felt the same again. It wasn't just that Papaw was gone. It was the erasing of him. Like a vindictive cleanse of the house. The swallowing up of every soft thing he'd left behind.

Even the air changed.

His scent of smoke and peppermint, replaced by lemon cleaner and low grumbles.

His flannel blanket was replaced by Nanny's rough crocheted one that scratched my knees.

Sometimes I closed my eyes and tried to remember the sound of his laugh. I was already forgetting the way it rumbled from his chest against my little ears.

I wish we had kept something. Anything. But grief had made her greedy.

And in her hunger, she stole not only prized possessions worthy of succession - she stole everyone's memories.

Spell for The Things That Disappear Too Quickly

Ingredients:

One memory you almost forgot
A drawer left empty
A scent that makes your chest ache
Silence thick as syrup

Directions:

1. Write down what you remember before it fades.

2. Hold it in your palm like it's still warm.

3. Whisper their name into the quiet.

> "I keep you in the spaces no one thinks to look.
> Between the heartbeats,
> behind the words,
> beneath the sadness.
> You are not lost.
> You are just hidden from her."

Repeat when need to hold on to the memories they want you to forget.

CHAPTER
Eight

Tectonic Shift

I was still a child, technically. But something was shifting. Not all at once, more like a soft, slow erosion. Like the ground beneath me had started to slope, and no one noticed I was sliding.

Mom was unraveling in quiet ways. Crying behind the shower curtain. Slamming the door to the bathroom and staying in there too long. Sleeping through alarms. Forgetting to pack my lunch. She wasn't mean, not like Nanny could be. But she was... disappearing. Even when she was still in the room.

Dad was working more. Or maybe just avoiding home altogether. My brother, nine years older, was mostly disassociated. Too far away in age, too far gone in his own world to notice mine cracking. He drifted back and forth between our house and Nanny's like a balloon with no lift - landing wherever the consequences were the fewest.

I didn't go to Nanny's much anymore - not like I did when Papaw was alive. But my house had stopped feeling like home, too. Everywhere felt like somewhere I didn't *quite* belong.

I learned to walk lightly. To keep my voice soft. To clean up before being asked. I thought if I was good enough, quiet enough, small enough, maybe things would stay steady. Maybe life would be easier.

Then came shame.

It didn't arrive all at once, just a shadow that started trailing me.

It happened after I started crying in the car - again. I don't even remember why. Something small, probably. Something about the music, or missing Papaw, or just feeling too full.

Mom's hands tightened on the steering wheel. Her voice cut through the soft hum of the road.

"Why do you always have to cry? You're too emotional. It's just so - *exhausting*."

Not cruel - just tired. But tired words can still bruise.

I pressed my face to the window, trying to catch the tears before they hit my cheeks. I didn't want her to see them anymore. I didn't want *anyone* to.

That's the day I started caring what other people thought of me. The day I learned to tuck it all in - to smile when I wanted to scream, to laugh when my chest ached.

That's how shame starts. It doesn't yell. It leans in close and tells you to shush.

Spell for When the Ground Begins to Shake

Ingredients:

One empty lunchbox, closed but echoing
A tear that never fell
A joke you didn't find funny
The sound of a steering wheel gripped too tight

Directions:

1. Find a quiet place where no one is watching. Sit with your back against the wall - the way you used to when the house felt unstable.

2. Open the lunchbox and whisper inside it:

> "This quake is not my fault.
> This silence is not my shape.
> I *am* allowed to feel."

3. Tap your heart once with your palm. Take three deep breaths in and out.

4. Close the lunchbox. Let the echo greet you next time you open an empty lunchbox.

Repeat when you feel yourself shrinking to fit a world too brittle to hold you.

CHAPTER
Nine

The Night The Clock Stopped Ticking

Grief doesn't whisper in a family like mine. It slams doors. It shatters glass. It digs its claws into whatever soft parts are left and drags them into the open.

My parents had been fighting more and more - not over anything specific, just the ache that grief leaves behind when it settles into the cracks of a home. Every missed look, every wrong word, became a spark. And our house was dry kindling.

I was in my room, trying to disappear - the way I always did when voices got sharp and syllables started to separate. I pressed my pillow over my ears, but the walls weren't thick enough to keep out the rising volume. Words like knives. Accusations hurled like stones. I waited for the quiet to return, like it always did. But this time, it didn't.

Instead, the silence broke differently. In a blood-curdling scream. I don't know why, but I wanted to see what caused this horrendous cry. I opened my bedroom door just as it happened.

As soon as the door swung open and I emerged, a sound rang out - *bang* - sharp and sudden, louder than any slammed door or dropped plate. Not a shout. Not a sob. A rupture. A *pop* that split the moment in half and echoed through my bones.

I stepped into the hallway, barefoot, heart thudding like a war drum. The air was thick - not with smoke, but with something worse. With the aftermath. My eyes scanned the living room too quickly, and then not fast enough.

There, to my right, on the carpet, was a weapon I had never seen before.

Still warm. Still humming with violence.

My father stood rigid, his chest heaving like it had forgotten how to breathe. My mother, on my left, was pale, her face slack with something deeper than fear. Her mouth was moving, but no sound came out. The words had died before they could form.

I had walked into the eye of something unholy - into the middle of grief with teeth. Whether it went off by accident or by intention didn't matter. It had been *brought out*. It had been *held*. It had been *ready* to shoot. And I had been just down the hall - a child orbiting the blast zone of two people too broken to protect what was left between them.

I didn't speak. I didn't cry. I just stood there - watching them examine my body like some alien creature. While I was watching the distance between them becoming permanent.

That night, I learned something awful. Love can arm itself and sometimes, it aims without blinking.

–

Christmas didn't feel like Christmas that year.

The tree stood crooked in the corner, a little bare on one side. The lights blinked unevenly, like they were trying to pretend nothing was wrong. There were gifts under the tree - not many, but enough for a child to believe, for one more year, that magic still came if you were good.

Mom made sure of that. She drained her savings, every last bit, just so we'd have something to open.

She smiled through gritted teeth, taking long sips from her toxic elixir between the wrapping paper tears. Dad sat stiff on the couch, barely looking up, his jaw locked like it hurt to speak.

It had been months, and no one talked about Papaw. Not really. Not out loud. His absence was too big to name - so we all just pretended it wasn't pressing down on the house, like snow on a sagging roof. It was our first Christmas without him, and the silence in his place made the room colder than it already was.

New Year's Eve felt like the end of something long before midnight struck.

Mom was in the kitchen, curling her hair in the microwave reflection, her drink can leaving a wet ring on the counter. She wore too much perfume and kept checking the clock. She wanted to go out. Dad didn't. He sat on the couch behind me, arms folded, remote in hand, flipping through channels without really watching, sulking over the money he'd lost gambling weeks prior.

I was on the floor between them, pretending to color in a book I didn't like, trying to disappear inside the lines.

"I told you I wanted to go out tonight," Mom said, loud enough for the whole house to hear. "It's New Year's. *Everyone* goes out on New Year's."

"You already went out," Dad muttered, not looking at her. "Spent all our money on Christmas like it'd magically fix something."

Her eyes flared. "*I* made Christmas happen. Who do you think paid for those presents? I used every last dime I had because you gambled away our Christmas. We almost didn't have one at all - because of you."

Dad finally turned his head. "Oh, please, you're far from perfect, Diana."

"No," she spat, "you made a choice. You gambled away Christmas. You gambled away all we had. I had to beg to keep the lights on."

"Don't act like you're so clean. You're a twelve pack in and it's not even ten o'clock."

I could feel the heat rising in the room. The kind that made your skin prickle. Like lightning was about to strike.

Mom slammed her can down on the counter, foam spilling onto her sleeve. "You wanna talk about clean? Let's talk about your *lies*. About how you were 'working on the road' for weeks at a time while I was at home with two kids and no heat!"

Dad stood. "I work to survive, not to drink it all away."

"You? Survive?" she laughed bitterly. "You sit on that couch like a corpse and expect everyone to call it living."

They spat back and forth for what felt like forever.

"I lost my father too - years ago, and I'm just fine, you need to get over it. Stop being so sensitive!" Dad snapped.

Silence hit like thunder.

That's when I knew - they weren't just fighting each other. They were battling their grief. And I was stuck in the middle of it, cross-legged on the stained carpet, gripping a crayon like it could protect me.

"I want to go out," Mom said, her voice brittle now. "I want one night to feel like a person again."

"And who's supposed to watch *her*?" Dad growled, gesturing towards me, pretending not to listen.

"You're already planted on the couch," she shot back. "Just stay there and keep an eye on her."

"I'm not your babysitter."

"You're right. You're her father. Now act like it."

He stared at her. She glared back.

And then he turned.

Walked right past me - I could smell his cologne and frustration.

"Where are you going?" she shouted as if she were offended.

"I'm done."

The door slammed. A car engine turned over. And just like that, the house changed shape.

I sat there a long time, until the heat from the argument cooled into silence. Mom slammed her bedroom door as I sat in the same place I was sitting when my dad walked out the door. I didn't budge. Maybe this was a bad dream?

After an uncomfortably long silence, I grabbed my coat and jelly sandals then ran through the cold to Nanny's house, feet crunching over old ice, lungs burning deep.

I banged on the door like I was being chased. My brother answered, taller now, already looking like a teenager. He was staying at Nanny's house more often than not at this point. It had been a few days since I had seen him last. And longer than that since I spoke to him last.

"Dad left!" I said. "He's gone."

He looked at me - really looked - and then shook his head.

"Stop crying. You don't know what you're talking about. Go home."

Then came the slam. Not just the door, but the feeling of it echoing down into my chest. I stood there a moment longer, breathing in the cold, hoping he might open it again.

He didn't.

The porch light didn't flicker. No footsteps followed. Just the echo of rejection and a winter wind that didn't care I was six.

I stood there, frozen - not just from the cold, but from the knowing. That bone-deep knowing that nobody was coming. Not now. Maybe not ever.

And then I felt it.

Not a hand. Not a voice. Just the presence - the familiar hush that slipped into the spaces others left behind. The Darkness.

It didn't frighten me this time. It wrapped around me like a heavy coat, like warm breath on icy skin. It didn't speak, didn't need to. It understood.

When the world went silent, it was the thing that remained. Not the parents. Not the brother. Not the house.

Just me.
And the Darkness.
Like we'd known each other a long, long time.

It didn't lead or follow. It walked beside me, step for step, down that cracked sidewalk, with the moonlit sky pressing low. We didn't speak. We didn't have to. My feet knew the way. And so did it.

When I reached the front door, I turned the knob with shaking hands and stepped back into a home that no longer felt like one. The furniture sat where it always had. My crayons are still on the floor. But I could feel it in my bones; *everything* was different.

Everything stood as it always had, except the golden clock on the entryway table. It had stopped working precisely at midnight. Midnight on New Year's. Frozen in time.

Like an omen that stepping into the New Year without my family was an impossible task. I glanced up from the broken clock to realize the entire room felt frozen in time, much like the broken clock that once ticked so loudly and gave this house a heartbeat.

My whole world had stopped in this instant. The ground was crumbling beneath me. I knew this was the beginning of the end. The end of my family. Regardless of the fractures that existed, this family was still mine, still worth holding on to, still worth preserving.

But was I the only one who saw this? Was I the only one who cared enough to desperately hold these broken pieces together?

The Darkness lingered by the doorway as I slipped off my shoes. Dripping from the ice that clung to them.

And I felt - just for a moment - not alone. Not safe and warm, but *known* and *held*. My parents had been married for eighteen years. And tonight, it all unraveled in a single event. Right before my very eyes.

Our home was falling apart. But the house was still standing.

And now, so was I.

Spell for When Time Stands Too Still

Ingredients:

One crayon - clutched too tightly
A slammed door still ringing in your ears
A porch light that never flickered back on
A clock stuck on midnight

Directions:

1. Sit in the quiet after the storm - not to silence it, but to hear what's left behind.

2. Hold the crayon in your palm. Let it remind you: even small things can leave marks.

3. Close your eyes and picture the ticking clock. Say the words:

> "Even when the hands won't move,
> Even when no one opens the door,
> Even when love leaves the room -
> I remain."

4. Breathe. In through what was lost. Out through what you're becoming.

Repeat when you need to remember that you didn't vanish with them.

CHAPTER
Ten

The Quiet Girl with the Loud Heart

The classroom smelled like glue sticks and pencil shavings, a scent that should've meant safety. Routine. Childhood. But for me, it was a place where I learned to split in two.

There was the version of me the teachers loved - polite, quiet, always coloring inside the lines. I kept my desk neat. I raised my hand. I smiled. And the smile was the most important part. It didn't matter if I'd cried myself to sleep the night before. As long as I smiled, I belonged.

But there was a side of me that the other kids found strange. They called me "crybaby" when I got overwhelmed. When I cried during a sad story or flinched at the sudden clang of a metal chair. When I sat still too long and stared out the window. When I wasn't loud like the other kids.

"Too sensitive," my mother whispered like it was something contagious. Like it would stain her if she touched it too long.

So I learned to hide it. To tuck my emotions behind perfectly written spelling words and fake coughs that earned me time in the nurse's office. She always treated me like a person. Asking how my day was going as we'd pass in the hall. The school nurse was a twinkling light in a darkening world for me.

At recess, I often stayed close to the wall. Other kids played tag and screamed like their joy had never been questioned. I wanted to join them. I wanted to scream too. But my scream was different. Mine wasn't born from fun. It came from something tangled deep in my ribs, something I didn't have the words for yet.

One afternoon, a boy knocked over my lunch tray in the cafeteria. It wasn't on purpose, just an accident - too many kids and too little space. But the crash of the tray, the splatter of applesauce on my pants, the laughter from the next table - it felt like too much. I started to cry, quietly at first. Then harder. My teacher crouched beside me, trying to calm me down.

"You're okay," she said. "It's not a big deal. Just calm down."

But it was. Not because of the food. But because I'd been holding everything else in. Because my father had left. Because Papaw was gone. Because the warmth of our house had drained out and no one seemed to notice. Or care that I was drowning in sadness.

One day in class, I was bent over in pain with a tummy ache. They sent me to the school nurse. She called my mom with no answer or a call back. She gave me Pepto Bismol and a soft voice. She had crayons in her office with white printer paper. I filled the sheets with reds and purples and greens. Colors I didn't understand yet, but felt like truth. I was drawn to the darker colors.

At home, when I tried to talk about anything that bothered me, Mom would sigh. "You're always crying over nothing. You've got to toughen up."

My mother stopped noticing things after Papaw died - or maybe she noticed, and just didn't care.

My brother, nine years older, moved through our world like a shadow - distant, unreachable. Detached. He didn't cry. He didn't yell. He didn't say much at all. Sometimes, I wondered if he noticed how heavy the house had become. If he saw me shrinking in the silence we all pretended wasn't there. But when I asked him questions, his eyes drifted past me with a muffled scoff under his breath. He had his own way of surviving - disappearing in plain sight.

Was no one truly on my side? Am I to go through life always feeling this lonely?

I missed my Papaw, I missed my family. I missed safety.

Most mornings, I woke myself in yesterday's clothes, wrinkled and stiff with the dirt of whatever hadn't been washed away. My socks never matched. My hair tangled overnight and stayed that way. Some days, I smelled like old food or the smoke that clung to the furniture. Some days I didn't smell like anything at all, and that scared me more - like I was fading from the world's notice, one unwashed day at a time.

Mom never asked if I'd brushed my teeth. Never checked my backpack for homework or lunch money. There were whole weeks when she barely looked me in the face. I'd wake up to the sound of her already halfway through her first smoke, the ashtray full from the night before. She'd mutter a reminder that school started in an hour, then disappear into the haze of her own life, her grief, her anger. I stopped expecting anything more.

But the nurse saw me.

She never said it outright, but I think she knew. She had to know that something in my world had tilted wrong. That the child showing up in the same shirt three days in a row wasn't just forgetful - she was being forgotten.

She kept clean clothes in her office. Not fancy ones. Just donated extras - soft sweatshirts, leggings without holes, socks that hugged instead of slouched. She offered them without pity. No big speeches. Just, *"Looks like you might be more comfortable in these."* She let me shower in the gym locker room when no one else was around. The water there was always too cold, and the lights too bright, but I didn't mind. It felt like someone cared, even if only for a moment.

Sometimes, she brought two lunches. She'd set the second one quietly on the counter when I came in after pretending to be sick.

"Too much math again?" she'd say with a wink.

I'd nod and peel open the sandwich slowly, savoring every bite like it was made of safety. I learned how to smuggle the fruit cups and granola bars into my backpack without anyone noticing. I saved them for the nights when dinner didn't happen - when Mom was too tired, too intoxicated, or too gone to remember I still needed feeding.

The nurse never pried. But her kindness pried something loose in me. A belief that maybe not every adult in my life had to hurt me or ignore me. Maybe some love came quiet, steady, and wrapped in clean socks and peanut butter sandwiches. She couldn't fix what was happening at home. But she made school survivable.

And sometimes, survival is the kindest spell a child can be offered.

Spell for the Forgotten Child

Ingredients:

One name no one ever says aloud
A photo face down in a drawer
Three sighs that never found their voice
A patch of moonlight that no one claims
Silence, aged and sharpened

Directions:

1. Begin at dusk. Not because it's magic - but because that's when the ache returns.

2. Find a quiet corner where no one has ever looked for you. Sit there until the air begins to hum.

3. Take the name you were given, the one they stopped using, and whisper it to the walls. Let the sound remind you.

4. Press your palms to the floor. Tell the Earth your story - not for justice, not for revenge - so someone knows. Even if it's just the floorboards.

> "I was never the problem.
> I was the spell they were too afraid to cast."

Repeat when you feel the world has forgotten you.

CHAPTER
Eleven

What Was Never Mine to Lose

It started with the sound of shifting boxes.

Mom was rearranging things again. Pulling open closets and slamming drawers like the chaos inside her needed a place to live outside, too. Her moods were quick like summer storms - fast, loud, and over before you could prepare. I'd learned to keep out of her way, to fold into the quiet corners of the house and make myself small. When Nanny wasn't around, she could be her true self. Even if her true self grew more bitter each passing day.

But this time was different. She wasn't just angry. She was unraveling.

Since Dad left, she had grown harder, thinner, like a thread stretched too far. Elixir cans began to stack like towers beside the couch. Different men came and went, some laughing too loudly, some never saying a word. I never learned their names. And they didn't learn mine. She didn't ask if I was okay anymore. She didn't notice if I was there at all.

She started wearing heavier makeup. Staying out longer.

Sometimes, never coming home at all. Laughing louder with strangers than she ever had with us. It was like she was trying to erase the life we had before - scribbling out one version of herself and replacing it with a woman who didn't remember bedtime stories or warm baths. The house didn't feel like ours anymore. It smelled different. Sounded different. Like the walls themselves were learning how to forget my family existed.

That's how I found it.

A rogue bouncy ball landed in the laundry room, and on my search and rescue mission, I found it. Tucked behind the dryer, buried in dust and lint - a chipped coffee cup I'd never seen before, but somehow recognized. The handle had been broken and glued back on, the ceramic etched with tiny cracks that spiderwebbed across the surface. There was a faded image on the front of a fish jumping from water, half-worn and ghostly. It definitely didn't belong here, much like I was feeling these days.

I didn't know how I knew, but I *knew*. This cup had belonged to Papaw. Then it clicked, I remember seeing Papaw sipping from it in old photographs at Nanny's house that hung on the walls still, despite her cleansing of his existence. And then it *must* have been given to Dad. I had faint memories of him sipping his black coffee from this mug when I was just knee-high to a grasshopper.

It smelled faintly of smoke and stale coffee. The kind of smell that wraps around memories and hides them from air and light, like something worth protecting. I traced the rim with my thumb and felt something settle in my chest - a connection not spoken, but sensed.

This was more than a cup. This was a thread.

I took it to my room and placed it on the windowsill. It

didn't do anything magical. It just sat there, heavy and humming. But I watched it like it might blink. Like it might remember something for me. I ran outside, down to the creek that ran on our property and gathered wild daisies to put inside this new special relic I have found. I wanted to bring a little bit of beauty back into the house. As soon as I crossed the threshold to my room, I arranged the daisies in the coffee cup and admired my wondrous creation.

My brother passed by the door and glanced in. He didn't ask what I was doing. He rarely did. He was already halfway gone from us - older, distant, living in his headphones and hollow silences. Our worlds barely touch anymore. He floated above it all, numb to the storm.

That night, Mom stormed in looking for an old receipt. She stopped when she saw the cup.

"Where did you get *that*?" she asked.

"It was behind the dryer," I said.

She stared at it. Her mouth flattened. "That old thing?"

She picked it up, turned it in her hand. The daisies spilled onto the floor without a care in the world. The glued handle cracked a little more under the pressure.

"This piece of junk?" she said. "There's no reason to keep this broken thing. You'll cut yourself."

She left the room with it.

I waited for the sound of the trash can lid. It never came. Just silence. A silence that told me it was gone. Whether thrown out or packed away, it didn't matter. It had been mine for a moment. And now it wasn't.

I sat on the floor, staring at the bare spot on the sill and the stepped-on wildflowers on the floor. My chest felt tight. That small warmth I'd carried from the laundry room to my bedroom had evaporated. It felt like *I* was the crushed daisies.

That's when I felt it. The cold.

Not a breeze. Not a chill. A *presence*.

It pooled in the corner of the room, a shadow that didn't belong to anything. Taller than before. Heavier. It didn't come with teeth or snarls. It didn't move fast. It just *was*.

Watching.

Waiting.

It was the chill from the storm. The same darkness from the funeral. From the walk home on New Year's. But now it was older. Bigger. Hungrier.

I didn't run. I didn't cry. I just pulled my knees to my chest and stared back. My breath fogged the air. The room had grown darker, even with the lamp on. It felt like the space between one second and the next had stretched thin.

The darkness didn't speak. But it didn't have to. I understood it now.

It came when something was taken.

It came when no one else saw the magic that still lingered.

It came without warning.

Spell for Magic No One Else Can See

Ingredients:

One object everyone else calls worthless
A memory that won't let go
A hush that lives between blinks
One breath held too long

Directions:

1. Sit with your back to the wall and your heart facing forward.

2. Hold the object, even if only in your mind.

3. Whisper to it: "I see you. I remember."

4. Let the magic rise, even if no one else believes it's there.

> "Some things don't need
> to be fixed to matter.
> Some things are powerful
> just by surviving."

Repeat until the quiet feels sacred, not empty.

CHAPTER
Twelve

Iron Grip

It was supposed to be just another weekend.

Dad had taken me to the flea market. We got greasy burgers wrapped in foil, and he let me pick a book from the clearance bin - the kind with a unicorn on the cover and all the pages water-warped.

For a moment, the world felt soft again. For a moment, I remembered what safety smelled like: coffee, leather seats, and a little bit of gasoline. Dad didn't talk much, but he smiled at me that day. That was *enough*.

Mamaw drove me back to Mom's house on Sunday night. She had the heat cranked up too high in her car, and the windows fogged as we pulled up the gravel driveway.

The house looked like it had been partying without us. There were unfamiliar cars in the grass, a broken folding chair near the porch, and a crowded ashtray on the steps. Inside, the walls echoed with laughter that didn't sound happy. The kind that didn't care who was listening.

When I saw Mom, I ran to her. My voice rushed out before

I could second-guess it.

"Can I stay with Dad *one more night*? School's out tomorrow. *Please*?"

She wasn't looking at me when she said yes. Just waved her hand like she was shooing a fly. "Whatever."

I smiled. I turned to grab my bag and ran back toward Mamaw's car. But before I could reach the driveway past the bushes, the tires shrieked. The tail lights blinked away.

She drove off. She didn't see me. She left me.

I screamed. I chased after her barefoot. My flip flops fell off in the chase, gravel biting into my feet, heart punching against my ribs.

"Mamaw! Come back! Please!"

I didn't understand. I still don't.

Mamaw was Dad's mother, everything Nanny wasn't. Soft-spoken, but never weak. Her hugs lingered, and her kitchen always smelled like coffee and banana bread. She was steady, calm, the kind of person you felt safe with even in silence. She never raised her voice, never raised a hand. It confused me, then, that she left me there. That she didn't stay. That she didn't wait.

My mother's footsteps caught up with me seconds later. Her grip was iron. She yanked me back by the arm, my feet pressing into the gravel as I screamed.

"Don't you *ever* run from me again," she hissed. Her breath was sour and sharp.

She dragged me down the driveway. Through the yard.

Past the crooked porch and toward the shed. The night air bit at my cheeks. The moon was thin and useless.

She threw open the door. A single lightbulb hung from the ceiling. It buzzed. It swung. And then it bore witness.

She threw me into the corner.

And then the beating began.

Closed fists. Open palms. Screams. Her rage had no shape, no logic. She wasn't hitting *me* in her mind. She was hitting every disappointment life ever handed her - and I was just the skin it landed on.

I balled up as tight as I could. Arms over my head. Knees to my chest. But the blows came fast. To my back. My sides. My legs. My face.

It felt like forever.

Until I heard another voice.

"DIANA! WHAT ARE YOU DOING?"

My aunt's scream cut through the fog.

Mom froze. Her fists loosened. Her breath came ragged and uneven. She stepped back like she'd just woken from a spell.

The shed fell silent except for the buzzing light and my soft, shaking breath.

My body ached in every place it could. I wouldn't be able to lift my arms for days. The bruises would turn from purple to green to yellow before they faded.

But I knew I had to be quiet.

The family made sure of that.

No one called anyone. No one told anyone. The next day moved on like nothing had happened. But *I* knew. *My body* remembered.

And so did the darkness.

It had appeared in the middle of the road as I chased Mamaw's car. A figure, tall and pulsing with something hot and angry fueling it. Not watching. Not waiting. *Following*.

It stood at the edge of the driveway as I was dragged away.

It pressed its shadow against the shed while the lightbulb flickered.

It darkened the room as she relentlessly wailed on my seven-year-old body.

This time, the darkness wasn't quiet.

It *growled*.

Low and thunderous, like a storm warning in your blood. The air felt electric. Alive. I felt it wrap around the walls, coiling, ready. It couldn't stop her, but it could bear witness. It could remember.

And that night, as I lay curled on the floor of my bedroom, I whispered a spell with a busted lip and a swollen eye.

Spell for When the Grip Is Too Tight

Ingredients:

A torn piece of fabric
A place you can be alone (closets count)
A candle imagined in your mind
One truth you're brave enough to whisper

Directions:

1. Sit in your chosen space. Let the quiet settle first.
Let it crawl into your lap like an old friend.

2. Close your eyes and light the candle in your mind.
Watch the flame dance. Watch how it never flinches.

3. Whisper this spell, even if your voice shakes:

> "This hurt is not mine to keep.
> These hands did not make me.
> This fear is not my forever.
> I am not the broken thing they tried to make."

4. Picture a door opening in your chest. Let the pain
walk through it. Let the darkness follow, not to haunt
you, but to carry what you cannot.

5. Blow out the candle (even if it was only pretend).
Let the silence say 'you survived.'

*"If they ever tell you it didn't happen, show them your
silence. Show them how even shadows remember."*

CHAPTER
Thirteen

The Vanishing Act

The days after the shed were made of silence. The kind that clings to your skin, your hair, your ribs. We didn't talk about what happened. No one did. Not Mom. Not my aunt. Not the neighbors across the road who surely heard something. Or the half-wit losers partying inside my house like they own the place - or maybe they did.

The bruises on my arms and legs bloomed like oil slicks, then slowly faded into a morbid rainbow of colors. I flinched when someone moved too quickly. I watched every doorway closely, like it might bite.

Life resumed, somehow. But the house felt heavier, like it was slouching under a weight no one else would name. My mother carried on like nothing happened, except she stopped yelling for a few days. She drank for breakfast. Sometimes she had company by noon.

There were always men. Three, mostly, who drifted in and out of the house like they lived there. I didn't know if they had names or just made-up ones. One had long hair and a mean laugh. Another slept all day and stayed up all night watching old westerns, shirtless and smoking. The third liked to call me "kid" and never looked me in the eye.

None of them were kind. None of them cared.

The house was filthy. Dishes stacked high and crusted. Floors gritty with dirt and bottle caps. The couch cushions sagged and smelled like sweat and ash. Trash piled near the back door in bags that no one bothered to take out. I wasn't cleaning it - I was living in it.
The bathroom was unrecognizable and made my stomach turn uncontrollably. Tiptoeing around messes like they were landmines. I was unsure if wiping the counters or picking up cans would provoke more anger. I didn't know what made people explode, only that it was usually something small.

I cooked a lot of my own meals. Toast. Canned soup. Crackers with peanut butter. I learned how to quietly close the squeaky cabinets, how to walk without making the floors creak. I was always trying not to wake something I didn't fully understand but knew would hurt me.

I tousled through laundry when I could, and sorted dirty dishes by which ones looked the cleanest. I tucked myself in at night. Sometimes, I turned on the radio just to hear another voice. Oftentimes, I would find myself watching 'Matilda' on repeat, resonating so deeply with the message that I too was a misunderstood, magical girl surviving in a family full of chaos. It gave me hope that maybe one day I would find my own 'Ms. Honey', and we'd live happily ever after having tea in the garden.

I was the most responsible person in that house. At seven years old. I was the only one who remembered I had a bedtime. I was the only one who remembered I needed food. I am pretty sure I was the only person who wanted to survive.

And I was lonely in a way that ate me alive every. Single. Day.

There were nights I sat on the floor with my back against my bedroom door just to feel close to someone, even if the voices behind the doors were slurred and mean. I would trace the lines in the wallpaper and try to imagine they were roads, leading somewhere else. Somewhere quieter. Somewhere warmer. I would imagine their laughs were from funny things I had said, or their voices were reading me a bedtime story. But I knew they weren't here for me.

My brother was above it all. Detached. Gone even when he was home. He didn't see me. Or if he did, he looked away. He stayed in his room mostly. I stopped knocking.

I still saw my dad on weekends. Those visits became small breaths in a long underwater week. But through the week, I lived with Mom, buried in the noise and the quiet, trying to find my shape in a house where I barely existed.

The darkness lingered.

It didn't always show itself, not like before. But I felt it. In the corners. In the silence. In the way the mirrors sometimes felt too deep, like they were looking back. It wasn't just watching anymore - it was waiting.

One night, I whispered to it.

"I know you're there."

And it moved.

Not a shape. Not a figure. Just a shift in the air, a shadow thicker than it should have been.

I wasn't afraid of it. Not anymore.

The people in my life had done far worse.

And when the house shook with the sound of laughter that wasn't joy, or when the front door slammed again at midnight, or when Mom stumbled through the hall smelling like sweat and smoke - I didn't cry anymore.

I just held my breath and let the darkness sit beside me.

Spell for Disappearing Without Leaving

Ingredients:

One can of cold soup
A sock without its pair
A radio playing low enough to whisper
Dust from under the couch
A hallway shadow that knows your name

Directions:

1. Sit in the doorway of your room. Right where the carpet thins from pacing.

2. Line up the ingredients in front of you. Don't speak. Just notice them. They're proof you existed today.

3. Whisper your given name like a question. Whisper it again like a fact.

4. Place your hand over your chest. If you feel anything at all - that's enough. That's the proof.

> "Even if they don't see me,
> Even if they never did -
> I am here. I am still here."

Repeat whenever silence becomes too loud.

CHAPTER
Fourteen

The Circus at the End of the World

She was already dressed when I woke up. Her hair curled, red lipstick applied with shaky precision. She smelled like poisonous elixir masked in cheap perfume, and she called me "baby" in that sing-song way she did when she wanted something.

"We're gonna have some fun today," she said. "The circus is in town."

I blinked at her from the couch, where I couldn't believe what I was hearing, still dressed in yesterday's clothes. For just a second, the word 'circus' felt like a bright thing in my chest.

Mom had won twenty bucks on a scratch-off ticket. She waved it like a golden ticket, declaring that she was finally going to do something nice for us. Something magical. She said I deserved it - for being "such a good girl."

But then the story shifted.

After a quick, hushed phone call, she said she was going

without me - just for a little while. She'll come back later tonight and we'll have the time of our lives. She had someone to meet and I was too little to tag along. "You wouldn't enjoy it anyway," she said. "It's going to just be grown ups talking, boring stuff, I'll come back to pick you up tonight for all the fun stuff. Don't worry, baby."

I nodded even though my throat closed. I watched her apply one more coat of mascara in the hallway mirror. She looked excited, flushed like someone on the edge of adventure.

She left with a flippant kiss on my forehead and the word 'circus' echoing like a song I wasn't allowed to hear.

She walked out into the night, heels clicking, smoke trailing behind her. I was left with silence and a buzzing television.

I didn't sleep much that night.

Instead, I sat by the window. I tried to imagine the circus: the smells of popcorn and sawdust, the shimmer of lights reflecting off sequins, the echo of laughter and trumpets and roaring lions. I traced out tents in my imagination, drew fire-breathers and trapeze artists flying high in the air.

I made my own circus out of dust bunnies and flashlight shadows. My stuffed animals watched from the couch, lined up like ticket holders. I did the voices. I played every part just right.

I never saw the circus that day. I wasn't ever meant to. It was hers alone - one more place I could imagine but never step into. I was already asleep on the couch when she stumbled in the door.

When she returned, she smelled like burnt popcorn and

stale lies. Her cheeks were flushed, and her lipstick had bled outside the lines.

"Too magical to describe," she slurred, kicking off her shoes.

So I imagined harder.

Because if I didn't, I'd have nothing.

Mamaw called the next morning. Said she was checking in and that she'd try to visit soon. She always sounded warm, like a fire burning on a cold night, even through the phone.

I wish she were the one who had taken me when Dad left.

She always smelled comforting. She folded her towels neatly. She looked people in the eye and was the exact opposite of the chaos I was learning to live inside.

But I didn't live with her. I lived with Mom, weekdays mostly. Dad had me on weekends, a split carved quietly after the holidays.

Sometimes, when it got quiet enough to hear my own heart, I turned the television on just to listen to the 90's TV moms who smiled too often and said things like, "Dinner's ready!" or cared about the problems their children were facing and stood by them as they found resolution to today's newest problem, together.

Something I had never experienced for myself.

I imagined they were talking to me.

I was walking towards my bedroom door when a glance into the disgusting kitchen suddenly caught my eye. The chipped coffee cup had sat forgotten on the counter. It had belonged to Papaw once, then Dad. It made its way through time like a survivor. I held it once, felt its weight, its story. But no one else seemed to notice. I grabbed it and hid it deep within my closet, safe from sight.

That night, I pressed it to my cheek. It was cold.

And in the far corner of my closet, just past the flicker of the television, the darkness stirred.

Bigger now. Bolder.

It didn't whisper. It watched. Like it had before.

Waiting.

Because it knew something even bigger and darker was waiting just around the corner.

Spell for When No One Is Coming to Save You

Ingredients:

One chipped coffee cup that still remembers warmth
A blanket pulled over your shoulders like a knight's cape
The glow of a flashlight under the covers
Three deep breaths taken while no one is looking
Your truest wish, a tiny whisper only the dust bunnies can hear

Directions:

1. Find a quiet corner - turn off every light except the one you made yourself - a flashlight, a TV screen left glowing, a night light shaped like a star.

2. Whisper to your stuffed animals. Line them up like witnesses. Give them names. Let them cheer for you.

3. Close your eyes and build your own circus - from dust, from shadows. Imagine lions roaring just for you. Imagine music that never lies. Imagine someone clapping just because you're brave.

4. Sit cross-legged, holding the chipped coffee cup in your palms. Feel its weight. Let it anchor you.

5. Now take three deep breaths. Inhale like you're

breathing in magic. Exhale like you're letting go of every lie they told you.

6. Hold your breath for one heartbeat more - long enough to feel the silence. Just long enough to know you're still here.

Touch your hand to your heart. Speak these words softly, like a vow only the dark can hear:

> "I am not nothing. I am not invisible. I am the whole show; the stars applaud me. I will keep building magic from broken things. Even if no one claps, I will still dance.
>
> Now open your eyes.
> If the darkness is still there, let it stay.
> Let it watch.

The circus belongs to you now.

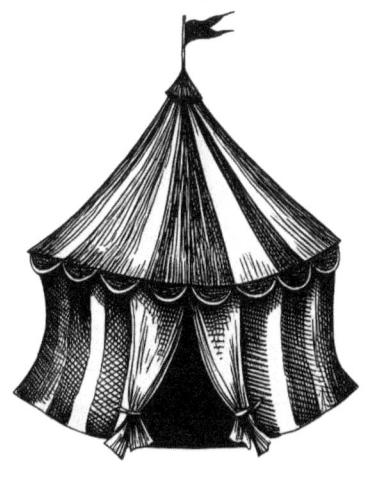

CHAPTER Fifteen

Smothering Fog

It started with yelling.

Not the usual kind that lived in the walls like mold - but something sharper. Something that cracked the night in half. I was seven years old and already learning how to listen like prey. When the tones changed when mom had 'friends' over, I knew to hide. But this time, I stayed frozen.

I was standing in the hallway, barefoot, the carpet rough under my toes. The living room was lit only by a crooked floor lamp with a red shade that made everything look like danger.

A man had my mother by the neck.

He shoved her so hard that the plaster behind her cracked. She hit the wall with a sound that didn't seem real. His voice thundered, a string of curses and demands I didn't understand. But I knew what they were doing. Even then, I knew what dangerous potions looked like - what danger felt like.

I couldn't move. My little hand clutched the wooden door

frame like it might save me.

She gasped. He let go, and she fell to the floor like a discarded doll. And then he was gone. Just like that.

She fell to the floor and lit a smoke with shaking fingers, her knees bent under her like a marionette dropped by its strings. She didn't even look at me. Just muttered, "He's just mad. It's fine, baby. Go back to bed."

But I knew it wasn't fine. I knew it in the part of me that had started to shape around fear. In the quiet, I backed away.

A few nights later, the house turned into a party again. The kind where the floor shook and the music tried to cover the truth. She was in a good mood - lipstick crooked, eyes too wide, drinks flowing. She told me to stay in my room. Told me to be good. Which I knew meant to stay unseen.

I was lying in bed with the TV on, pretending to be asleep if any sounds passed my doorway. My bedroom door didn't lock. At first, I heard the twist of the doorknob, which always made a loud pop, unless you know EXACTLY how to open it just right, like I did. I was an expert at remaining unheard in my home.

I saw the illuminated outline of the door shift, so I closed my eyes and turned over, facing the wall quickly and quietly. The light bouncing off the wall grew slightly brighter for just a quick moment, faint footsteps, then the door crept shut with quiet intention. I could sense I wasn't alone. I could smell that I wasn't alone. The scent of smoke and sweat encompassed my room like a pungent candle being lit. That night, a man I didn't know came into my room and invaded my space.

He stepped lightly towards me, tripping over my toys that

littered my floor. His voice was slurred. I don't remember what he said, or if he said anything at all. I do remember, however, his shadow stretching across the wall like a fresh wound.

He brushed my hair as if he were someone to trust. He laid his hand against my chest to feel the rise and fall of my breath. He stayed in that moment for a while. I'm sure he could feel my little heart beating out of my chest. Then he touched my leg, lightly at first. But his hand traveled too far.

I froze.

I didn't scream. I didn't speak. I just closed my eyes and disappeared inside myself. Wishing this moment was a dream.

And that's when the darkness returned.

Not the kind that comes from the absence of light - but the living kind. It gathered in the corners of the ceiling, watching. Then it bled down, slow and thick. The air turned heavy and strange, like I was breathing underwater.

The fog poured in from nowhere - cold and silver and humming.

It didn't whisper. It remembered me.

It pressed against my chest where this dark stranger's hand once pressed, wrapped itself around my limbs, like a baby being swaddled. My eyelids grew heavy. My breath slowed. The room went soft around the edges, like a picture losing focus.

And I sank - not to sleep, exactly, but somewhere quieter. Somewhere *underneath*.

Like a dream that forgets your name on purpose.

I woke with light crawling through the window and a taste like I had slept with a penny in my mouth. The rain was pouring outside my window, but the fog was gone - so was the darkness.

Even if my mind tried not to, my body remembered. Everything.

Later that week, I looked into the bathroom mirror after a shower at the school gym. The glass fogged over, but when I wiped it away, there was no reflection staring back. I was gone.

Just a white space of nothing. And in that blankness, the fog whispered again.

"I'll be here when you need me."

Spell for When the Air Gets Too Thick to Breathe

Ingredients:

One mirror fogged over with silence
The outline of your body in the dark
A breath you forgot you were holding
The memory of your name, hidden in a corner

Directions:

1. Sit somewhere dim, somewhere quiet. Let the room blur at the edges.

2. Close your eyes. Inhale slowly, as if the air weighs more now. Exhale like you're trying not to wake the house.

3. Picture the fog. Let it come. Let it wrap you up. Let it see you.

4. When your chest starts to tighten, place your hand flat against your heart. Feel the proof.

5. Whisper, even if only in your mind:

> "I am still here.
> Even when the room forgets me.
> Even when my voice won't come.
> Even when I disappear to survive-
> I am still here."

Repeat any time the air gets too heavy.

CHAPTER
Sixteen

She Was Already Gone

She packed fast.

The smell of poisonous potions and stale perfume still hung in the air as she shoved clothes into a duffel bag and shouted over the phone to someone waiting for her. She said she got a job with the traveling circus. Said it like it was a grand promotion. Like leaving this life was a privilege she'd earned.

I stood in the doorway, bare feet cold against the warped linoleum. I watched her zip her life away. She didn't look at me when she said I'd be staying with Nanny for a while. Said it like she was doing me a favor.

She had already changed. Elixir bottles rattled in the trash, and new faces came and went from our house with unfamiliar names and laughing mouths. Her eyes were distant even when they landed on me. If they landed on me.

The day she left, there was a storm in the air. Not the kind that brings rain, but the kind that makes everything feel like it could break.

She dragged boxes to the front door while her boyfriend revved the engine in the driveway. I stood on the front steps, hugging my stuffed dog, heart pounding. Her packed bag thumped onto the passenger seat, and she adjusted her eyeliner in the mirror like she was going to a show.

"Almost ready?" her boyfriend called out.

She gave the house one last glance. But not me.

The build-up felt like hours. Her movements slowed. Her voice grew louder. My heart beat faster. I wanted to ask her to stay, but I didn't know the words.

The car door slammed. She didn't look back.

"Be good," she tossed over her shoulder as if she'd be back in an hour with a gallon of milk.

I didn't answer.

The fumes trailed behind her like a ribbon as the car peeled out of the driveway, tires spitting gravel. And just like that, she was gone.

I didn't ask questions. I didn't cry. I just waited for her to leave, so I could figure out what came next.

When the door finally slammed behind her, I didn't sit down. I grabbed my school bag, shoved in a toothbrush, my stuffed dog, and the cracked coffee cup that had once belonged to Papaw, then Dad.

And I walked.

To Nanny's.

The house stood like a forgotten statue, sagging at the bones, blind windows watching my approach. I climbed the steps with my backpack slung low and my heart even lower. Before I could knock, the door creaked open.

Nanny stood in the doorway, lit from behind by the flickering hallway bulb. She didn't look surprised. Just tired. Already disappointed.

She looked me up and down, then stepped aside without a word.

As I crossed the threshold, the smell hit me - mothballs, stale and clinging, mixed with fried grease and lemon cleaner. A scent like time giving up.

I paused in the hallway, waiting for some kind of greeting, or maybe a question. Instead, she sighed and muttered, half to herself, half to me:

"Your daddy left, now she's run off... and I'm stuck with you."

Her voice wasn't angry. Just resigned. Like I was the echo of a choice she never made.

The walls were yellowed by years of smoke and silence. The air heavier. And Nanny was worse now. Way worse.

Whatever grief had hollowed her during Papaw's funeral had calcified into something harder - something hateful and mean. Her mouth - a thin line, her eyes - sharp and assessing. Her sadness - no longer soft; it had grown brash and brittle.

She didn't ask why I was there. Just nodded toward the back room and muttered, "Put your things down."

She didn't mention my mother. She didn't ask if I was okay.

In contrast to my house, hers was clean. Immaculate, even. The scent of bleach stung the air, and the floors gleamed with a shine that dared you to step wrong. But it wasn't a comfort - it was a warning.

She cleaned to keep grief from swallowing her whole. And she hated children's messes. She would blare old love songs from the living room stereo in fits of a cleaning rage. She hated my presence, as if my very being reminded her of all that had been lost. She resented that my father had left, that my mother had vanished into smoke, and that she was left with me.

Her least favorite person in the world.

I didn't clean the house. I lived in it. I learned early that tidying could be mistaken for judgment, and judgment provoked fury. I became a shadow. I moved quietly. I did my homework on the floor.

My brother didn't speak much to me. He was older, already disassociated, detached from the rot. When I knocked on his door that first night, wanting to tell him Mom had left, he stared at me like I was speaking a foreign language.

I turned and walked back through the hall, past the peeling wallpaper and flickering overhead light. The smell of lemon scented cleaner and something older clung to everything. I returned to the living room, where the shadows gathered in the corners like waiting beasts.

My home was falling apart. But the house was still standing.

Dad still picked me up most weekends. Quiet drives, fast

food, and a borrowed calm. But through the week, this house was my new map. One I didn't choose.

Sometimes, when the television worked, I'd turn it on low just to hear voices. I imagined the mothers on sitcoms were mine. They cooked casseroles and wore soft sweaters. They hugged their children. They asked about homework.

Nanny did not ask about homework.

She asked about chores. About silence. About why I was wasting electricity.

And the darkness?

It became the only thing I could count on to be there consistently.

It took shape in the living room first, an oily presence that pooled in the corners where the light didn't reach. It swelled with the tension in the house, grew bolder with every slammed cupboard, every insult left to ferment in the air.

It wasn't a whisper anymore. It was a weight.

When I sat on the couch, it sat with me. When I stared at the porcelain dolls, it loomed.

It was in the shadows, but not of them. A thing with shape and breath, with the patience of something ancient.

It fed on abandonment. It fed on silence. And it was eating me alive.

That night, I held the chipped coffee cup in my hands and whispered the only thing I had left.

Spell for When They
Leave Without Looking Back

Ingredients:

One ribbon dropped on the road
A stuffed dog - hugged too tightly
The echo of a slammed door
The silence after footsteps fade

Directions:

1. Sit by the window where you last saw them. Let the light (or the darkness) fall on your face.

2. Wrap the ribbon around your wrist. Not to remember them - to remember you.

3. Hold the stuffed dog in both hands. It's heavy with memory. It will not break. Neither will you.

4. Whisper to the air, to the ghosts, to yourself:

> "You left.
> But I stayed.
> And still, I rise."

Repeat as needed - especially when it feels like their leaving was your fault.
But just remember, it never was.

CHAPTER
Seventeen

What the Rain Remembered

I turned eight without a sound.

No streamers. No singing. No arms reaching for me in love or celebration. Just a grocery store cake with my name smudged and no one at the table to sing me through it. No parents. No candles. Just a waxy number 8 tipped over in pink icing, and the steady hum of a fridge louder than the voices in the room.

My brother had gotten a pool party for his birthday at the hotel Nanny managed - balloons, presents, too-sweet punch in clear cups. His laughter bounced off the indoor pool walls like something that had never been broken. I stood at the edge of the water that day, not jealous exactly. Just absent. Like I'd wandered into a memory that didn't belong to me.

When my day came, no such world was built around me.

It was a birthday without presence - or presents. No celebration. Only reminder.

Nanny didn't even look up when she handed me the

cake. "Go ahead," she said flatly, motioning at the box like it offended her. Then she turned her attention back to her number puzzle book.

I picked at it in silence. The frosting was dry. The center still cold from the refrigerator. I didn't finish my piece.

Later, I heard her on the phone with my father, voice sharp and just loud enough for me to overhear:

"Come get your daughter. I didn't take this girl to raise. I can't take it anymore." I froze. I'd always known I wasn't exactly wanted here. But some truths cut deeper when spoken aloud.

Living with Nanny was cold in every way a place could be. The floors were hard linoleum, slick and angry beneath my feet. When I hurt myself - once, slicing my heel open on a jagged tile edge of the pantry - she didn't ask if I was okay. She snapped at me for bleeding.

"Don't you dare drip blood on my clean floors. I just mopped this morning. Get out of here."

So I limped to the bathroom alone and learned not to cry too loud.

But trauma doesn't sleep forever.
It waits. It remembers. And that summer - so did the rain.

The heat broke open one evening - thick clouds pressing low like grief too swollen to hold itself together. I sat on the porch, knees pulled tight to my chest, watching Papaw's old rocking chair sway gently in the wind.

It shouldn't have moved. There was no one in it. But it rocked anyway - just enough to notice. Just enough to hurt.

The rain started as a whisper. Then a murmur. Then a sob. It wept against the world in long, aching streaks, each drop a memory trying to crawl its way back inside.

That's when the mist came. It seeped from the edges of the porch like memory turned vapor - slow, silver, curling. Familiar. The way dreams do when you try to explain them out loud.

It moved like breath on glass. Like something not quite alive, but not dead either.

And in it - the figure.

The Darkness had changed again. It was no longer a chill up my spine or a shadow to bear over me. The mist had become a shape. His shape. The dark stranger - the one who entered my room the night of the party while my mother laughed and music rattled the walls. The one who took something I didn't yet have the words to name.

He stepped forward through the fog, not real but not gone, either - more memory than man now. His silhouette bloomed and blurred, his presence filling the air like smoke from a fire long buried but still burning underground.

And behind him, the mist played its cruel theater:

Papaw's casket being lowered into the ground.
My father walking out the front door, keys in hand.
My brother's back as he shut Nanny's door in my face.
My mother's voice laughing in a room I couldn't leave.
The sound of footsteps and a strange, heavy breathing.
The loud boom that split my soul in two.
The silence that followed.

I reached for the porch railing to steady myself. My fingers were cold. My mouth tasted like metal and sorrow.

I didn't cry. I didn't scream. I just watched.

Because that's what children do when no one protects them. They watch and remember.

And the rain? It remembers everything, too.

The moment was broken by Nanny's shrieking demand to go check the mail. Of course, she would tell me to do this now. In the pouring rain.

I jetted across the front yard, grabbed the mail, and set back towards the house, jumping puddles along the way. When I reached the front door steps, I glanced down at what I had just retrieved like a good little girl.

It was a single postcard. Addressed to *me*. With a picture of a ringmaster on the front. I flip it over.

"See you soon."

Spell for When You Feel
Like No One Cares

Ingredients:

A single candle no one bothered to light
The silence after a missed birthday
One strand of mist (imagined or remembered)
A drop of rain saved in memory's palm
Your name, spoken only in your own voice

Directions:

1. Find a quiet space. A porch. A stairwell. A bedroom corner.
Somewhere that knows your stillness.

2. Sit with your knees to your chest and press one hand
against your heartbeat. Not to stop it - just to prove it's still
there.

3. Close your eyes. Let the forgotten moments rise. Let
them speak.

4. Whisper this, aloud or inside:

> "Even if no one lit the candle,
> I am still a flame.
> Even if no one called my name,
> I shall remain.
> The rain remembers.
> The mist mourns.
> And I will forever endure."

You are enough.
You always have been and you always will be.

CHAPTER
Eighteen

Tightrope

The postcard only said, '*See you soon*'.

No return address. No explanation. Just my mother's handwriting, in red ink, curving sharp like a secret. But that was all it took.

For days, I carried that message in my pocket like a promise. I ran my thumb over the ink until it smudged. I imagined what "soon" meant. Tomorrow? A week? A minute from now, if I closed my eyes hard enough?

I distinctly imagined where she was - the circus. Not the kind you find in parking lots. No, this one lived in my mind - my mother's circus - glimmering, golden, untouchable.

There were soaring trapeze artists, faces aglow with bravery. Glittering girls in sparkling tights twirled batons of flame. Lions roared from gilded cages with manes like thunderclouds. Acrobats flew like angels over nets woven from moonlight. Every lightbulb shimmered like stardust. It was where magic lived, and she had gone ahead to make it ready for me.

At least, that's what I told myself. Because anything less would mean she left me for something worse. And how could that be true?

The day finally came. Dad picked me up in silence. No radio playing. No complaints about traffic. He just drove. And that silence was thick - like even he knew this moment mattered.

The traveling circus sat on the edge of town, parked like a tired dream. From far away, the tents still held shape. The faded stripes still whispered possibility. I tried not to notice how the flags drooped or how the signs peeled like sunburnt skin.

When we arrived, I expected someone to greet us, to sweep me into that world of wonder. But no one did. Dad walked with me as far as the entrance, then paused. "You want me to come with you?" he asked.

I shook my head no. This was supposed to be just between her and me.

Inside, the illusion unraveled quickly. The air stank of mildew and wet straw. The animals looked tired - ribs showing through matted fur, eyes sunken like old buttons.

The rides creaked mournfully, turning slowly as if even they were reluctant to keep moving. Everything was smaller than I'd imagined. Duller. A fairground of almosts, has-beens, and not-quites.

I walked past clowns whose face paint had cracked, performers who smoked between acts, eyes sunken and teeth yellowed. The magic had long since left the building.

And then I saw her. My mother. Draped in a scarf patterned with stars, red lipstick smeared like a broken promise. She stood among a cluster of other carnies - jugglers and too-skinny women with crooked grins. When she saw me, her face lit up like I was part of the show.

"There she is!" she called out, loud enough for everyone to hear. "My girl! My pride and joy!"

She grabbed my hand with that iron grip like we'd always been close. "This is my daughter," she said, turning to the group. "A real good kid. Loyal. Sweet. Always been my little shadow." I didn't say a word.

She paraded me around the grounds like she was giving me a tour of paradise. She pointed to sagging tents and rusted rides like they were relics of a lost kingdom.

"This here's the tiger cage," she laughed, even though there were no tigers, just a few hunched dogs panting in the shade. "That's where we do the knife-throwing act," she added. Her voice pitched higher with every step. She was selling this place - selling herself - like a used car salesman trying to unload a lemon with four bald tires and a cracked windshield.

"This is where I belong," she said at one point, her eyes darting to the others nearby. "This life, it's real. None of that nine-to-five. We live on our own terms out here."

I didn't say anything until we reached the far edge of the grounds, past the porta-potties and the sagging tent with holes big enough to let the sky peek in. I stopped walking. She turned around, still smiling, but it was weaker now. I looked her dead in the eyes.

"Why?" was all I asked. Just one word.

Her smile altered. "What do you mean, baby?"

"Why this?"My voice cracked, but I didn't care.

"Why did you leave me for this?" I said. "You said you were coming back. You said we were gonna have magic. But you came here instead. And look at it - look at them!" I motioned to the hunched figures, the trash, the whole hollow mess of it all.

Tears flooded my eyes like a baptism. It was like I could finally see. For the first time, I wasn't looking for excuses or answers. I was looking through her.

I saw the truth:

My mother wasn't a mythical creature chasing freedom.

She was a woman who abandoned her child for a rotting dream.

She wasn't someone to idolize.

She wasn't even someone to pity.

She was someone I would never, ever become.

I knew then - I would never leave my child behind.

I would never settle for scraps and call it 'freedom'.

I wanted more.

I deserved more.

I was going to be MORE.

Spell for Walking the Line Between Fantasy and Truth

Ingredients:

One soggy postcard
A lion with no roar
A piece of frayed rope
A child's question left unanswered

Directions:

1. Stand at the center of your disappointment. Let it tower over you. Let it rot.

2. Breathe in the mildew from the scent of the postcard and make it your proof.

3. Tie the frayed rope around your wrist - not to hold you back, but to remind you.

4. Say aloud:

   "I saw it all. And I still chose better."

Repeat whenever the fantasy calls you back.
Remember - you are not the one who disappeared.

CHAPTER
Nineteen

Good Knight

I packed everything I owned into grocery bags. A couple of shirts, my stuffed dog, my notebook, a hairbrush with half the teeth missing that I had as long as I could remember. A pair of shoes too small but still mine. I didn't have much, but I had enough to leave. And oh boy, I was ready to leave!

Dad waited in the driveway, his old truck humming like it was just as ready as I was. The sky was the kind of blue that looks like possibility. I didn't cry when I left Nanny's house. I didn't look back, either.

"Ready, baby girl?" he asked, pulling open the passenger door for me like it was my royal chariot to the ball.

I nodded eagerly. Climbed in and buckled up.

And just like that, we were flying north on the highway - away from every familiar ghost and into something I could almost believe better.

He smiled more than I'd seen in years. Played country songs on the radio, the kind that talked about fishing and freedom and long roads home. He even rolled the window down and let me stick my hand out into the wind, letting it ride the air like a bird.

We stopped at a diner on the way. One of those little roadside places off Highway 11 with booths that stuck to your legs and coffee that smelled stronger than it tasted.

He ordered a burger, told the waitress - a woman with a crooked smile and bubblegum pink nails - that it was the best thing on the menu. He flirted with her a little, just enough to make her laugh and swat his shoulder. I watched him become someone else for a moment. Confident. Charming. Lighter.

He told me old army stories over French fries. About sneaking into mess halls, sleeping under stars, and pulling pranks on his buddies. He promised we'd go fishing soon - something he loved more than I did, but I said yes anyway. Anything to be with him. Anything to stay by his side.

He talked about the house up north like it was a castle. Said it had a yard, a little porch, even a room just for me.

"You'll love it," he said. "It's not fancy, but it's ours."

Ours.

I clung to that word like a raft. It had been so long since I'd belonged to something.

The ride felt like a dream. Every tree we passed, every gas station and rest stop, pulled me further away from the old me - the forgotten girl with ghosts in her closet and dirt on her shoes.

I was going to be new. Going to be safe. Going to be *his*.

I reached into the glove compartment and found an old

gas station map. I held my tongue out as I folded it into a little makeshift crown. Wore it like a badge of hope.

Dad looked over and laughed.

"You always were my princess."

And in that moment, I believed it.

Spell for Taking a Leap of Faith

Ingredients:

One folded paper crown
A shoelace knotted with hope
The first French fry shared across a booth
A mile marker that feels like a new beginning

Directions:

1. Buckle your heart. Roll down the window.

2. Let the past fall behind you like dust.

3. When you see the road curve north, whisper:

> "Not all knights wear armor.
> Some drive old trucks
> and call you baby girl."

Repeat as needed. Especially when doubt starts to whisper again.

CHAPTER
Twenty

Leave The Light On (As Something Waits In The Shadows)

The gravel crunched beneath us as we pulled into the trailer park. It was smaller than I imagined - just a scattering of aging mobile homes clinging to one another like old secrets. But when Dad said, "We're home," I believed him.

The trailer was single-wide, sun-faded and rust-kissed, but it had a porch light that flickered just slightly as we approached, like it had been waiting for us. A warm hello.

Inside, everything was cramped - but instantly, it felt like mine. My room had just enough space for a twin mattress and a milk crate that doubled as a nightstand. A single window looked out over a patch of gravel and weeds. I unpacked my grocery bags carefully, placing what little I owned in tidy rows.

It was the first time in a long time that I had a space of my own that didn't feel borrowed. As I sifted through my few belongings, I realized my stuffed dog I slept with at night must have gotten left behind at Nanny's. 'No worries,' I thought, 'I'm sure I'll get it when I visit next time, plus, maybe now I can get a *real* dog.'

I sat cross-legged on the floor and imagined the life ahead of us. Dinner at the table. School projects on the counter. Laughter from the TV. I imagined years unfolding quietly and sweetly in this little space we called ours. No more screaming matches. No more slammed doors. No more whispers through walls or locks that didn't work. No more walking on eggshells. Just me and Dad. Safety.

For a few weeks, it was like that.

We went to the gas station and picked out snacks just because we could. We made scrambled eggs and toast in the morning. He told me I could add anything I wanted to the walls. I drew out big dreams in my notebook - plans for a corkboard with photos of all the new friends I'll make at my new school, ideas for new routines, and planned events together.

The life of a bachelor and his daughter - a place where bedtimes were rarely on schedule, but memories were being made. The good kind of memories, though, the kind worth remembering. Not like the last two years have been. This was going to be different.

The Darkness wasn't gone, not completely. I'd catch it sometimes in side-glances, in the corners of mirrors, or flickers at the end of the hallway. Sometimes it felt like a trick of the light, sometimes like a whisper I couldn't quite make out. But I told myself I didn't need it anymore. I was good now. *We* were good now.

We began developing slow, meaningful rituals. Mondays were spent at Mr. Gatti's, a fun place that served pizza and pasta, but had a full arcade in the back of the restaurant. We played weekly UNO matches, and he loved to paint my nails anytime I requested it. I truly felt like a princess here.

We were standing outside one Sunday evening when she pulled up, just as the sun dipped below the tree line. My dad smoothed his shirt and said, "Now that's a woman. You'll like her. She's real special." I wanted to believe him. And I did. At first.

She stepped out of her car like a caricature, a specimen I had never seen before with my own two eyes - sharp heels, red lips, bleach-blonde hair that glowed unnaturally under the sunlight. Blue eyeshadow arched like war paint, and nails long enough to scratch the truth out of someone. Her name was Reta.

The wind picked up. Cold and sudden - in mid-July. And then I saw it - not her, but *behind* her. In the trees. *The Darkness*. Not a flicker this time. Not a passing trick of the light. It stood there, watching.

Like it had arrived with the wind. Like it had followed her here. Like it already knew something I didn't quite understand.

It didn't speak. It didn't move. But it made itself seen. Was this impending danger? Was this a warning? I couldn't tell. Not yet.

She reached out and pinched my cheek too hard. Her perfume was thick and sweet, but in a way that wrapped around your throat and didn't let go.

"Well, aren't you just precious?" she cooed. But her eyes never matched her mouth. I smiled because my dad was smiling. I smiled because I wanted this to work.

But deep down, I knew - this was the end of something soft.

And the beginning of something else entirely.

Spell for When You Want to Believe

Ingredients:

One porch light, left on for you
Three brave wishes whispered into a pillow
The tiniest room where hope can grow
A shape you almost don't see

Directions:

1. Step into the space made for you.

2. Name it "home," even if your voice shakes.

3. Let the light touch your skin and say, "I am safe here."

4. When the shadows return, do not greet them. Let them pass like the weather.

> "Some spells don't chase the dark away.
> They teach you how to bloom *without* light."

Repeat any time you're feeling lost and alone.

BORN TO CARRY BOTH

There are rooms I never meant to return to -
  Memories I tiptoed past like broken glass,
  Names I carried like bruises under long sleeves,
  And homes I left before I ever got the chance to leave.

But I did not vanish.
  I did not disappear into the cold.
  This book began in snow,
  In a silence so loud it could drown a child.

And yet-
  I clawed my way through every blizzard,
  Every hallway that held more haunt than home,
  Every grief that curled itself around my ankles
  And tried to convince me I belonged beneath it.

But I rose.

And I am still here.
  Still spelling my way forward,
  Letter by letter, breath by breath.
  Still learning how to name myself with love
  Instead of survival.

Still believing in soft things-
  Even after being shaped by sharp ones.

If you've made it this far,
  Maybe you, too, are part of the spell.
  Maybe you've held your breath in dark places.
  Maybe your story isn't finished either.

Let this be your reminder:
  The darkness may know your name-
  But so does the light.

And some of us-
  We were never meant to choose between them.
  We were born to carry both.

THE AUTHOR

Barbara Latinka is a first-time author, photographer, wife, and mother of three. For years, she carried this story in silence-until now. With a voice forged in survival, Barbara brings her truth to the page with honesty, grit, and empathy. She shares what it means to grow up shadowed by the darkness, how to find magic in the normalcy, and how surviving sometimes looks like strange spells.

When she's not behind the lens or with her family, she's writing words that turn wounds into spells and shadows into poetry.

This is her debut work - and just the beginning of a longer spell in the making.

CONTINUE THE JOURNEY:

SPELLS *for* SURVIVING a HAUNTED CHILDHOOD

PARTS TWO & THREE

AVAILABLE NOW
www.HauntedLight.com

Resources for the Wounded, Watchful, and Healing

No matter how dark your story has been, *you are not alone.* I encourage you to self-reflect, place yourself in a positive environment surrounded by positive influences, and get into see a therapist for talk therapy.

A special thank you to Donna Lockaby,
www.lockabycounseling.com

If you are reading these pages and feel a familiar ache-if your childhood mirrored even a fraction of what's written here-I want you to know that help exists. *Healing is possible.* You are never too broken, too late, or too far gone to reclaim your light. *Never.*

If you are witnessing someone else in danger-say something. Report it. Protect the child. Be the adult you wish someone had been for you. You could save a life.

There is power in reaching out, even if your voice trembles.

Below are resources where trained professionals are ready to listen, support, and help you take the next step:

NATIONAL RESOURCES (U.S.)
Childhelp National Child Abuse Hotline
1-800-4-A-CHILD (1-800-422-4453)
childhelphotline.org
Available 24/7. Free. Confidential. For survivors and those concerned about a child's safety.

National Domestic Violence Hotline
1-800-799-SAFE (7233)
Text: START to 88788
thehotline.org

RAINN – Rape, Abuse & Incest National Network
1-800-656-HOPE (4673)
rainn.org
24/7 confidential support for sexual assault survivors.

National Suicide & Crisis Lifeline
Dial or Text: 988
www.988lifeline.org

IF YOU'VE WITNESSED ABUSE:
If someone is in immediate danger, call 911.

To report suspected abuse or neglect, call Child Protective Services in your state.

You can also contact Childhelp at 1-800-4-A-CHILD for guidance on how and where to report.

Always Remember:

You are never a burden.
You are not too much.
You are NOT the things they did to you.
You are becoming.
You are rising.
And help is just one brave whisper away.

You've got this. I believe in you.